Transform Your Life Through Mindfulness and Chakras

Alan G. Pierce

Contents

Contents

Chapter One

INTRODUCTION

Mindfulness can change your life for the better.

Release Subconscious fear and taking back the present

In this case, the name of Melissa A. Holloway is

Welcome to the world of Transform Your Life through Mindfulness. Thank you for downloading it.

In the next few chapters, we'll talk about the principles and history of mindfulness. This class will teach how to use mindful living in your daily life. You will learn about the history and meaning of mindfulness, and then how you can use it in your daily life. Mindfulness is a practice that can change your life and make a lot of things better, so let's start.

Thanks again for picking this book. There are a lot of books on this subject out there. If you find it useful, please enjoy! HIStory

An easy way to explain the history of mindfulness is to say that it comes from Buddhism. Around 2,500 years ago, the Buddhists began to meditate, and this led to what we now call "mindfulness." To reach inner peace, unlock their own abilities and grow their concentration, intellectual abilities and spiritual development they used meditation, which is also called "prayer."

It was already a long time ago when Buddha was born. Mindfulness was already a part of the Hindu way of life and how they taught things. During Buddha's teachings, he used the idea of mindfulness as the main point. Life was all about it, and he explained what that meant for people in the real world. Buddha had a lot of people who kept track of what he said. Jesus didn't have that many people.

During the next two thousand years, Buddhism spread all over India and a lot of the Far East, like China and Japan. When it spread to new places, the religion would take in the local religion and culture. This gave the religion a lot of new flavors and colours. The Shamanistic Ban religion had an impact on Tibetan Buddhist thought and ceremonies. This is how Taoism and Confucianism influenced Chan Buddhism when it moved from Japan to China. The Japanese culture had a big impact on Japanese Zen.

These different types of influences could be neutral or even good for the original effects of mindfulness, and then some of them could be bad for the body and mind. People who practice Buddhism think that women are less important than men. Those who are teaching them make the women think that they can't become wise. They make them think that they can only hope to be born as men in a second life. Some people in Tibetan cultures still believe that these ideas are true.

Mindfulness is still thought to be an important part of the Buddhist faith. It takes a lot of time and effort, and only people who have studied under a Buddhist teacher can teach it to other people. People who don't take the time to learn how to use and practice mindfulness will fall down on their own.

As the Christian religion has faded in the West, a different culture has grown instead. Spiritualists and theosophists started to appear in the early 20th century. Allan Ginsburg and Bob Dylan led the beatniks in the late 50s, and then in the 60s, it was the hippies, who were a new group. Today's culture is open to alternative beliefs, green ideas, psychology, and a wide range of religious thought.

A lot of people in the West now like Eastern culture. There are three main types of meditation: Japanese Zen, Thai Vipassana, and Tibetan Buddhist meditation. This is why people in the West are interested in these teachings. They see them as a kind of mystic, and they call them "Non-Returners" or "Enlightened People."

These live-in Buddhist centers started to appear in the United States and Europe in the 1960s and 1970s. They were mostly found in Europe. This is how people like The Beatles, Timothy Leary, and Ram Dass spread the word about these places: through media attention and books.

There was a bigger source of these teachings before the internet came out because of it. With the help of YouTube, websites, and forums, Buddhist teachings began to spread around the world. Meditation was used to treat emotional problems in psychotherapy and counseling in the past. It has made it into the public eye over the last few years. Public health services say it's good for you. There is a good chance that the spread of mindfulness is because it is simple.

In the modern world, a lot of people are interested in the psychological and medical benefits of mindfulness. Good news: There is a lot of research that shows that mindfulness and yoga can, in fact, help people with a lot of different mental problems and improve their health. MINDFULNESS

No, I haven't. When I get to work, I don't remember any of the car ride. Have you ever finished a bag of popcorn and you didn't even know you had opened it? Most people have been in situations like this at some point in their lives. A lot of people don't pay attention, or they go on autopilot.

During most of the day, most people are on autopilot. When you are on autopilot, you become absorbed in your thoughts, which makes you not be present in your life. Some people think that autopilot is like being in a dream because you don't pay attention to what is going on in the present moment.

Every day, it's easy to lose yourself for most of the day. The problem is that when you're on autopilot, you don't get to enjoy the beauty of the world around you as much as you should. Body language: You don't pay attention to what your body is telling you. You're stuck in the same old ways of living, and your body is telling you. Most of the time, when you're in autopilot, you don't think about what you're doing and just keep going. Because you are always trying to get things done, you don't have any time to enjoy life!

These feelings build up and get worse. Getting your mind off of things and going on autopilot makes you less happy, it has been shown. This leads us to being mindful, which is what we want to do.

When you're mindful, you're the exact opposite of mindless. It is the act of waking up and taking charge of your attention. The goal of mindfulness is to stay aware of everything that is going on around you at all times. This includes your body, thoughts, feelings, and surroundings. It also means that you don't judge people. The first time you start paying attention, you can't judge what you think or feel. Make sure you don't care about anything.

People who are mindful are meditating in a way. As you meditate, you pay attention to the way your breath moves through your body. When you pay attention to your breath, you can pay attention to your thoughts as they come to mind and then let go of things that you are having trouble with. People have these thoughts all the time, but they don't make them. You can think of your thoughts coming and then popping, like a bubble, as they go away. There is only a short time for good and bad feelings and thoughts. They happen and you have control over whether you act on them.

I don't think about what I'm seeing. You have to be kind and not be mean to yourself. When you're stressed or unhappy, you'll learn how to treat it like a dark cloud and watch it move away, instead of taking everything personally. There are a lot of ways that you can learn how to control your negative thoughts so that they don't send you into a downward spiral. It gives you the power to be in charge of your own life.

The way you pay attention will change in three main ways when you start to be more mindful. Keep your attention...

On purpose

When you practice mindfulness, you are doing so deliberately and consciously. With autopilot, your attention is constantly bombarded with a never-ending, and mostly negative, thought process. When you use mindfulness you wake up and are able to remove yourself from that current and control where you want your attention. You become more conscious. You live consciously and are more awake.

You immerse your attention in the...

Moment

If you let your mind work on its own, it will naturally wander around and not focus on the present. It will get stuck on thinking about the past and the future. Your mind, on its own, is never really present. With mindfulness, you are wholly in the present. You experience the here and now. You release the tension that is built up by the need for things to be different or wanting more. Instead, you are able to accept things as they are.

Lastly, you hold your attention...

Non-Judgmentally

With mindfulness, you are not trying to suppress or control your thoughts. You are trying to pay attention to the things you experience when they come up without labeling them in some way. It will allow you to be a watcher of emotions, sense perceptions, and thoughts. You no longer get caught up in your current emotions and allow them to sweep you away. When you become a watcher you won't be as likely to play out things that have happened to you or will happen to you. It gives you a freedom from your own thoughts.

The longer you practice mindfulness the more long-term changes you will notice. Your happiness, well-being, and mood will all improve. Studies have proven that this kind of meditation can prevent depression and improve anxiety and stress levels. You will learn how to deal with irritability and emotional stressors more easily. Many other studies have proven that people that meditate won't see their doctors as often as others, and won't spend as much time in hospitals. Your memory will also improve and you will have a faster reaction time.

Even though there are lots of benefits to mindfulness, that have been proven, people are still leery of the word meditation. Let's look at some myths of mindfulness.

Mediation and religion are not the same thing. Mindfulness is a way to train your mind. Lots of religious people practice meditation, but agnostics and atheists meditate as well.

There is no need to sit on the floor, cross-legged, but that is an option. You can also sit in a chair to meditate. Mindfulness is not limited to where you sit. You can bring it to wherever you are, train, bus, car, or walking. You are able to meditate wherever you are.

Meditation does not take up a bunch of your time. It does, however, take some persistence and patience. Lots of people realize that meditation can liberate them from the worry and stress of time. They find that they have more time to spend on more fun things in their life.

Mindfulness meditation does not have to be hard. It is also not about failure or success. You will have times when it feels difficult, but even then you will learn something from the experience. You learn how your mind works, giving you psychological benefits.

It won't make your mind go numb causing you to veer off of your lifestyle or career goals. You also won't become some brainwashed follower. It doesn't mean you have to accept the unacceptable. It only means that you will be able to see the world in a clearer way. It allows you to be wiser and take more knowledgeable actions in your life and allows you to be able to see a smarter path for your goals.

Basically, when you are mindful you are:

Not judging things that you notice, and you don't label things

You concentrate on the things that are around you on purpose

You try to avoid thinking about the things that have happened, or that might happen to you

You focus on the present

Humans spend so much of their life thinking about things that have already happened, trying to find ways that they could have avoided something, or constantly worrying about things to come, that they aren't able to appreciate what is right in front of them. Mindfulness gives you the ability to bring yourself to the present moment. You will be able to:\s

Cope with your stressors and stress

Relax

Concentrate more fully

Slow the nervous system

Slow down the thought process

Become more aware of the environment, body, and yourself

Clear the head\sWho Can Mindfulness Help

Mindfulness is a practice that anybody can develop, and anybody is able to try it. It has been in practice for thousands of years and has spread across the world. Anybody is able to increase mindfulness within their life through yoga and meditation, or by paying attention to things while doing regular everyday activities like brushing your teeth. BENEFITS

Mindfulness meditation can help with exhaustion, stress, irritability, depression, and anxiety when regularly practiced. It can also help improve your memory, your reaction time will become faster, and your physical and mental stamina will increase. Basically, you will become an overall happier person, and you will be less likely to end up suffering from any psychological problems.

Mindfulness can also help to reduce pain and the reaction to pain. Some of the recent studies have suggested that unpleasant pain levels may be reduced up to 57 percent in beginner meditators. Studies have also shown that it can help the quality of life and mood of people that suffer from back pain and fibromyalgia, as well as chronic disorders like IBS, and in challenging illnesses like cancer and multiple sclerosis.

Mindfulness is also capable of improving your memory, attention span, and creativity. It can also increase your emotional intelligence.

Mindfulness can also reduce the risk of self-destructive behavior and addiction. This means abusing prescription drugs, illegal drugs, and alcohol.

Mindfulness increases the gray matter in the brain which is associated with awareness, control, empathy, and attention. It helps to soothe stress hormones and increase the parts that lift the mood and helps to learn. It can also slow down the aging process of the brain.

Mindfulness can also reduce cellular aging and help the resilience of your chromosomes. It can also improve your circulatory and heart health. It can reduce blood pressure and hypertension.

As you have probably figured out, mindfulness can help you in lots of areas of your life. There are so many benefits that they all couldn't possibly be covered in this book, but I will cover some of the biggest benefits that mindfulness will give you.

Stress Reduction

As you know, mindfulness helps a large array of health conditions, and, for some reason, the reduction of stress seems to be a commonality. When stress and a less active prefrontal cortex occurs, it is considered very problematic. When you practice mindfulness, you will have more conscious control of the prefrontal cortex, which is what may be reversing the way the brain works with under stress.

That's why it makes sense that regular mindfulness practice would help to lower cortisol levels, which is the stress hormone. This is why experts believe that the stress reduction factor of mindfulness is the reason why it is so helpful.

Basically, mindfulness can help reduce stress and its markers. This is a big plus because stress can exacerbate other health problems.

Empathy

Have you ever found yourself wondering how somebody like the Dalai Lama is able to stay compassionate and kindhearted? The reason is likely in his mindfulness meditation.

In a study performed by Northeastern University, they found that a brief meditation during the day caused the participants to become 50 percent more compassionate. In a 2008 study published in PLOS ONE, non-experienced and experienced meditators, that practiced compassion meditation, had more brain activity in the areas where empathy is controlled. Anxiety and Depression

It's common knowledge that mindfulness directly affects mental health. There is strong evidence showing its benefits for suffers from general anxiety disorder and depression; the top two mental health conditions.

People that suffer from anxiety experience excessive, chronic, and very often uncontrollable worry. The sad thing is, almost 60 percent of anxiety patients won't improve with the use of conventional help, like psychotherapy and medications. The good news is; mindfulness is able to help those patients.

In one study, they took 89 anxiety sufferers and split them into two groups. One went through eight weeks of Mindfulness-Based Stress Reduction, and the other group went through eight weeks of regular stress management.

People of each group that was a part of at least one session showed improvement. In the end, the mindfulness group experienced greater improvement. Several other studies have proven more benefits when anxiety medication is used with mindfulness practice.

People who suffer from clinical depression experience low moods and they normally avoid regular activities. Depression is normally treated with psychotherapy or medication, but many patients will end up relapsing or they don't follow their medication regimen.

Mindfulness is able to keep people from relapsing when they don't want to use antidepressant drugs.

In a study on the effects of mindfulness and depression; a group of 28 patients received antidepressants to maintain their depression, another group of 26 patients was slowly taken off of medication while enrolled in a mindfulness-based cognitive therapy, and the third group of 30 patients that were taken off of their medication and given a placebo.

When the first two groups were compared to the placebo group, the first two showed a lesser likelihood of relapse. Remember that the mindfulness group was no longer taking any antidepressants.

Mild and moderate sufferers of depression receive the same benefits from antidepressants and mindfulness. This doesn't mean that you should stop taking your depression medication, that can be very dangerous depending on your level of depression, but mindfulness does give you an alternative to medication.

Intelligence

A UCLA study discovered that people that regularly meditated have more gyrification. Gyrification is the folding of the brain's cortex. The folds allow people to process information faster. They can also keep the meditator from dwelling on what has happened in the past, which in the end causes a distortion of thinking and decision-making process. In as little as 15 minutes of focused breathing, you can get out of your own head, get rid of the bias, and allow you to think clearly.

Reduces Loneliness

J. David Creswell led a study that looked at 40 older adults who meditated for 30 minutes a day over an eight-week time period, and found that their loneliness decreased. This is a huge discovery because a decreased feeling of loneliness along with more resilience and compassion

enables an individual to live a full, happy, and fulfilled life.

Weight Loss Obesity rates have increased globally in the previous 36 years. People are currently attempting to develop a method for treating and preventing obesity. Mindfulness may be beneficial since it has been shown to minimize stress-related overeating. Additionally, it may assist in increasing awareness of hunger; this is referred to as mindful eating.

A research discovered a link between mindfulness and a decreased risk of obesity, but they were unable to demonstrate that mindfulness decreased body weight. While some data from tiny clinical studies provide valuable knowledge, they are insufficient to draw a firm conclusion. It is reasonable to believe that mindful eating may help prevent obesity and promote weight reduction.

Attention and Concentration

By freeing the mind of distractions, mindfulness has been found to increase people's attention spans. In a 2008 brain scan research, it was discovered that the brain scans of Zen meditators revealed brain activity in several areas of the brain associated with spontaneous ideas. They discovered that the brain was able to revert to its Zen state despite being distracted for an extended period of time, in contrast to the brains of those who had not practiced meditation. The capacity of a person to concentrate on dull tasks was also greatly increased.

Sex Life You may be asking how this is accomplished; by bringing your thoughts into the present now. According to 2011 study, mindfulness training may assist women improve their sexual experience. It is usual for a woman's head to be filled with self-judgmental speech during sex. This prevents them from fully experiencing the experience. Additionally, they discovered that women in college who meditated were sexually aroused more quickly than women who did not meditate.

Risk Factor for Metabolic Disease

The phrase "metabolic syndrome" refers to a collection of symptoms that increase your risk of diabetes and cardiovascular disease. A person with three or more of the following is considered to have metabolic syndrome by doctors:

Hypertension

Following a fast, elevated glucose levels

Insufficient HDL

Excessive triglycerides

A waist circumference of more than 40 inches for males and more than 35 inches for women

Several observational studies have shown that those who practice mindfulness have a lower chance of developing metabolic syndrome. Several clinical investigations have examined the causal association between metabolic risk and mindfulness. The intriguing part is that although metabolic risk decreased, there was no substantial weight reduction.

In a clinical research involving 196 obese people, one group got simply exercise and nutrition counseling, while the other group received both as well as a mindfulness retreat. When compared to the first group, the mindfulness group had significantly lower triglycerides and cholesterol levels after

12 months and significantly higher glucose levels after 18 months.

Other research have shown that mindfulness may improve blood pressure, heart rate, and exercise capacity in persons with heart disease. They are still puzzled as to why these alterations occur. Researchers believe it may be related to changes in the autonomic nerve system, which regulates heart rate, blood pressure, and breathing.

Increased Calm

Paul Ekman, a pioneer in the field of emotion research, and Richie Davidson, a neurologist, researched Lama Oser, the Dalia Lama's right-hand man and a monk with over 30 years of meditation experience. They noticed that they could not record his left to right prefrontal brain activity ratio. The activity ratio indicated that he had extraordinary levels of serenity, resistance to setbacks, and well-being. This was entirely due to his mindfulness practice.

Bruises and Aches

These different types of influences could be neutral or even good for the original effects of mindfulness, and then some of them could be bad for the body and mind. People who practice Buddhism think that women are less important than men. Those who are teaching them make the women think that they can't become wise. They make them think that they can only hope to be born as men in a second life. Some people in Tibetan cultures still believe that these ideas are true.

Mindfulness is still thought to be an important part of the Buddhist faith. It takes a lot of time and effort, and only people who have studied under a Buddhist teacher can teach it to other people. People who don't take the time to learn how to use and practice mindfulness will fall down on their own.

As the Christian religion has faded in the West, a different culture has grown instead. Spiritualists and theosophists started to appear in the early 20th century. Allan Ginsburg and Bob Dylan led the beatniks in the late 50s, and then in the 60s, it was the hippies, who were a new group. Today's culture is open to alternative beliefs, green ideas, psychology, and a wide range of religious thought.

A lot of people in the West now like Eastern culture. There are three main types of meditation: Japanese Zen, Thai Vipassana, and Tibetan Buddhist meditation. This is why people in the West are interested in these teachings. They see them as a kind of mystic, and they call them "Non-Returners" or "Enlightened People."

These live-in Buddhist centers started to appear in the United States and Europe in the 1960s and 1970s. They were mostly found in Europe. This is how people like The Beatles, Timothy Leary, and Ram Dass spread the word about these places: through media attention and books.

There was a bigger source of these teachings before the internet came out because of it. With the help of YouTube, websites, and forums, Buddhist teachings began to spread around the world. Meditation was used to treat emotional problems in psychotherapy and counseling in the past. It has made it into the public eye over the last few years. Public health services say it's good for you. There is a good chance that the spread of mindfulness is because it is simple.

In the modern world, a lot of people are interested in the psychological and medical benefits of mindfulness. Good news: There is a lot of research that shows that mindfulness and yoga can, in fact, help people with a lot of different mental problems and improve their health. MINDFULNESS

No, I haven't. When I get to work, I don't remember any of the car ride. Have you ever finished a bag of popcorn and you didn't even know you had opened it? Most people have been in situations like this at some point in their lives. A lot of people don't pay attention, or they go on autopilot.

During most of the day, most people are on autopilot. When you are on autopilot, you become absorbed in your thoughts, which makes you not be present in your life. Some people think that autopilot is like being in a dream because you don't pay attention to what is going on in the present moment.

Every day, it's easy to lose yourself for most of the day. The problem is that when you're on autopilot, you don't get to enjoy the beauty of the world around you as much as you should. Body language: You don't pay attention to what your body is telling you. You're stuck in the same old ways of living, and your body is telling you. Most of the time, when you're in autopilot, you don't think about what you're doing and just keep going. Because you are always trying to get things done, you don't have any time to enjoy life!

These feelings build up and get worse. Getting your mind off of things and going on autopilot makes you less happy, it has been shown. This leads us to being mindful, which is what we want to do.

When you're mindful, you're the exact opposite of mindless. It is the act of waking up and taking charge of your attention. The goal of mindfulness is to stay aware of everything that is going on around you at all times. This includes your body, thoughts, feelings, and surroundings. It also means that you don't judge people. The first time you start paying attention, you can't judge what you think or feel. Make sure you don't care about anything.

People who are mindful are meditating in a way. As you meditate, you pay attention to the way your breath moves through your body. When you pay attention to your breath, you can pay attention to your thoughts as they come to mind and then let go of things that you are having trouble with. People have these thoughts all the time, but they don't make them. You can think of your thoughts coming and then popping, like a bubble, as they go away. There is only a short time for good and bad feelings and thoughts. They happen and you have control over whether you act on them.

I don't think about what I'm seeing. You have to be kind and not be mean to yourself. When you're stressed or unhappy, you'll learn how to treat it like a dark cloud and watch it move away, instead of taking everything personally. There are a lot of ways that you can learn how to control your negative thoughts so that they don't send you into a downward spiral. It gives you the power to be in charge of your own life.

The way you pay attention will change in three main ways when you start to be more mindful. Keep your attention...

On purpose

When you practice mindfulness, you are doing so deliberately and consciously. With autopilot, your attention is constantly bombarded with a never-ending, and mostly negative, thought process. When you use mindfulness you wake up and are able to remove yourself from that current and control where you want your attention. You become more conscious. You live consciously and are more awake.

You immerse your attention in the...

Moment

If you let your mind work on its own, it will naturally wander around and not focus on the present. It will get stuck on thinking about the past and the future. Your mind, on its own, is never really present. With mindfulness, you are wholly in the present. You experience the here and now. You release the tension that is built up by the need for things to be different or wanting more. Instead, you are able to accept things as they are.

Lastly, you hold your attention...

Non-Judgmentally

With mindfulness, you are not trying to suppress or control your thoughts. You are trying to pay attention to the things you experience when they come up without labeling them in some way. It will allow you to be a watcher of emotions, sense perceptions, and thoughts. You no longer get caught up in your current emotions and allow them to sweep you away. When you become a watcher you won't be as likely to play out things that have happened to you or will happen to you. It gives you a freedom from your own thoughts.

The longer you practice mindfulness the more long-term changes you will notice. Your happiness, well-being, and mood will all improve. Studies have proven that this kind of meditation can prevent depression and improve anxiety and stress levels. You will learn how to deal with irritability and emotional stressors more easily. Many other studies have proven that people that meditate won't see their doctors as often as others, and won't spend as much time in hospitals. Your memory will also improve and you will have a faster reaction time.

Even though there are lots of benefits to mindfulness, that have been proven, people are still leery of the word meditation. Let's look at some myths of mindfulness.

Mediation and religion are not the same thing. Mindfulness is a way to train your mind. Lots of religious people practice meditation, but agnostics and atheists meditate as well.

There is no need to sit on the floor, cross-legged, but that is an option. You can also sit in a chair to meditate. Mindfulness is not limited to where you sit. You can bring it to wherever you are, train, bus, car, or walking. You are able to meditate wherever you are.

Meditation does not take up a bunch of your time. It does, however, take some persistence and patience. Lots of people realize that meditation can liberate them from the worry and stress of time. They find that they have more time to spend on more fun things in their life.

Mindfulness meditation does not have to be hard. It is also not about failure or success. You will have times when it feels difficult, but even then you will learn something from the experience. You learn how your mind works, giving you psychological benefits.

It won't make your mind go numb causing you to veer off of your lifestyle or career goals. You also won't become some brainwashed follower. It doesn't mean you have to accept the unacceptable. It only means that you will be able to see the world in a clearer way. It allows you to be wiser and take more knowledgeable actions in your life and allows you to be able to see a smarter path for your goals.

Basically, when you are mindful you are:

Not judging things that you notice, and you don't label things

You concentrate on the things that are around you on purpose

You try to avoid thinking about the things that have happened, or that might happen to you

You focus on the present

Humans spend so much of their life thinking about things that have already happened, trying to find ways that they could have avoided something, or constantly worrying about things to come, that they aren't able to appreciate what is right in front of them. Mindfulness gives you the ability to bring yourself to the present moment. You will be able to:\s

Cope with your stressors and stress

Relax

Concentrate more fully

Slow the nervous system

Slow down the thought process

Become more aware of the environment, body, and yourself

Clear the head\sWho Can Mindfulness Help

Mindfulness is a practice that anybody can develop, and anybody is able to try it. It has been in practice for thousands of years and has spread across the world. Anybody is able to increase mindfulness within their life through yoga and meditation, or by paying attention to things while doing regular everyday activities like brushing your teeth.

If you are continually battling neck, back, or other physical issues, a portion of the problem may be psychological. According to a 2011 research, 80 minutes of mindfulness may almost halve the experience of pain.

Another research conducted by the University of Montreal corroborates this. They evaluated 13 meditators who had all completed 1,000 hours or more of meditation and compared them to non-meditators to see if meditation had any influence on pain perception. Finally, the meditators had a higher pain threshold than the others.

Microbiome of the Gut

If you weren't previously aware, your body is now infested with microorganisms. These are the microbes that comprise your microbiome. The majority of these bacteria reside in the gut or large intestine. When your microbiome becomes imbalanced or altered, you may suffer weight gain, impaired immunity, and inflammation.

They discovered a link between stress hormones and psychological stress, as well as their influence on microbial alterations in the intestines, in a few modest investigations. This indicates that mindfulness-based stress reduction may be able to prevent detrimental microbiota alterations.

Symptoms of Irritable Bowel Syndrome

IBS is a widespread ailment that affects around 7% to 10% of the world's population. Nobody knows for certain what causes IBS, but experts feel that it is likely caused by a combination of events. They hypothesize that psychological distress, stress, and digestive imbalances may be to blame.

Given that mindfulness may assist with all three likely primary triggers, it seems reasonable that it can assist in managing IBS. In a study of 43 patients, it was discovered that those who received mindfulness training saw a greater decrease in their symptoms. Even six months later, the advantages remained.

Diseases of the Nervous System

According to a study conducted by doctors at Beth Israel Deaconess Medical Center, the brain alterations associated with mindful meditation may help prevent the advancement of cognitive illnesses such as Alzheimer's and dementia. After eight weeks of mindfulness stress reduction, the Alzheimer's patients in the research had a slower deterioration in cognitive capacities than the control group. Additionally, they demonstrated a rise in well-being, which aids in recuperation.

Pregnancy

Stress during pregnancy has been linked to a variety of unfavorable outcomes, including low birth weight, preeclampsia, and hypertension. Several studies have shown that it may help alleviate pregnancy-related stress.

In a five-week trial of 74 pregnant women, a portion of the participants got twice-weekly mindfulness sessions. They demonstrated a greater decrease in stress than the other group.

Chapter Two

Excessive triglycerides

A waist circumference of more than 40 inches for males and more than 35 inches for women

Several observational studies have shown that those who practice mindfulness have a lower chance of developing metabolic syndrome. Several clinical investigations have examined the causal association between metabolic risk and mindfulness. The intriguing part is that although metabolic risk decreased, there was no substantial weight reduction.

In a clinical research involving 196 obese people, one group got simply exercise and nutrition counseling, while the other group received both as well as a mindfulness retreat. When compared to the first group, the mindfulness group had significantly lower triglycerides and cholesterol levels after 12 months and significantly higher glucose levels after 18 months.

Other research have shown that mindfulness may improve blood pressure, heart rate, and exercise capacity in persons with heart disease. They are still puzzled as to why these alterations occur. Researchers believe it may be related to changes in the autonomic nerve system, which regulates heart rate, blood pressure, and breathing.

Increased Calm

Paul Ekman, a pioneer in the field of emotion research, and Richie Davidson, a neurologist, researched Lama Oser, the Dalia Lama's right-hand man and a monk with over 30 years of meditation experience. They noticed that they could not record his left to right prefrontal brain activity ratio. The activity ratio indicated that he had extraordinary levels of serenity, resistance to setbacks, and well-being. This was entirely due to his mindfulness practice.

Bruises and Aches

These different types of influences could be neutral or even good for the original effects of mindfulness, and then some of them could be bad for the body and mind. People who practice Buddhism think that women are less important than men. Those who are teaching them make the women think that they can't become wise. They make them think that they can only hope to be born as men in a second life. Some people in Tibetan cultures still believe that these ideas are true.

Mindfulness is still thought to be an important part of the Buddhist faith. It takes a lot of time and effort, and only people who have studied under a Buddhist teacher can teach it to other people. People who don't take the time to learn how to use and practice mindfulness will fall down on their own.

As the Christian religion has faded in the West, a different culture has grown instead. Spiritualists and theosophists started to appear in the early 20th century. Allan Ginsburg and Bob Dylan led the beatniks in the late 50s, and then in the 60s, it was the hippies, who were a new group. Today's culture is open to alternative beliefs, green ideas, psychology, and a wide range of religious thought.

A lot of people in the West now like Eastern culture. There are three main types of meditation: Japanese Zen, Thai Vipassana, and Tibetan Buddhist meditation. This is why people in the West are interested in these teachings. They see them as a kind of mystic, and they call them "Non-Returners" or "Enlightened People."

These live-in Buddhist centers started to appear in the United States and Europe in the 1960s and 1970s. They were mostly found in Europe. This is how people like The Beatles, Timothy Leary, and Ram Dass spread the word about these places: through media attention and books.

There was a bigger source of these teachings before the internet came out because of it. With the help of YouTube, websites, and forums, Buddhist teachings began to spread around the world. Meditation was used to treat emotional problems in psychotherapy and counseling in the past. It has made it into the public eye over the last few years. Public health services say it's good for you. There is a good chance that the spread of mindfulness is because it is simple.

In the modern world, a lot of people are interested in the psychological and medical benefits of mindfulness. Good news: There is a lot of research that shows that mindfulness and yoga can, in fact, help people with a lot of different mental problems and improve their health. MINDFULNESS

No, I haven't. When I get to work, I don't remember any of the car ride. Have you ever finished a bag of popcorn and you didn't even know you had opened it? Most people have been in situations like this at some point in their lives. A lot of people don't pay attention, or they go on autopilot.

During most of the day, most people are on autopilot. When you are on autopilot, you become absorbed in your thoughts, which makes you not be present in your life. Some people think that autopilot is like being in a dream because you don't pay attention to what is going on in the present moment.

Every day, it's easy to lose yourself for most of the day. The problem is that when you're on autopilot, you don't get to enjoy the beauty of the world around you as much as you should. Body language: You don't pay attention to what your body is telling you. You're stuck in the same old ways of living, and your body is telling you. Most of the time, when you're in autopilot, you don't think about what you're doing and just keep going. Because you are always trying to get things done, you don't have any time to enjoy life!

These feelings build up and get worse. Getting your mind off of things and going on autopilot makes you less happy, it has been shown. This leads us to being mindful, which is what we want to do.

When you're mindful, you're the exact opposite of mindless. It is the act of waking up and taking charge of your attention. The goal of mindfulness is to stay aware of everything that is going on around you at all times. This includes your body, thoughts, feelings, and surroundings. It also means that you don't judge people. The first time you start paying attention, you can't judge what you think or feel. Make sure you don't care about anything.

People who are mindful are meditating in a way. As you meditate, you pay attention to the way your breath moves through your body. When you pay attention to your breath, you can pay attention to your thoughts as they come to mind and then let go of things that you are having trouble with. People have these thoughts all the time, but they don't make them. You can think of your thoughts coming and then popping, like a bubble, as they go away. There is only a short time for good and bad feelings and thoughts. They happen and you have control over whether you act on them.

I don't think about what I'm seeing. You have to be kind and not be mean to yourself. When you're stressed or unhappy, you'll learn how to treat it like a dark cloud and watch it move away, instead of taking everything personally. There are a lot of ways that you can learn how to control your negative thoughts so that they don't send you into a downward spiral. It gives you the power to be in charge of your own life.

The way you pay attention will change in three main ways when you start to be more mindful. Keep your attention...

On purpose

When you practice mindfulness, you are doing so deliberately and consciously. With autopilot, your attention is constantly bombarded with a never-ending, and mostly negative, thought process. When you use mindfulness you wake up and are able to remove yourself from that current and control where you want your attention. You become more conscious. You live consciously and are more awake.

You immerse your attention in the...

Moment

If you let your mind work on its own, it will naturally wander around and not focus on the present. It will get stuck on thinking about the past and the future. Your mind, on its own, is never really present. With mindfulness, you are wholly in the present. You experience the here and now. You release the tension that is built up by the need for things to be different or wanting more. Instead, you are able to accept things as they are.

Lastly, you hold your attention...

Non-Judgmentally

With mindfulness, you are not trying to suppress or control your thoughts. You are trying to pay attention to the things you experience when they come up without labeling them in some way. It will allow you to be a watcher of emotions, sense perceptions, and thoughts. You no longer get caught up in your current emotions and allow them to sweep you away. When you become a watcher you won't be as likely to play out things that have happened to you or will happen to you. It gives you a freedom from your own thoughts.

The longer you practice mindfulness the more long-term changes you will notice. Your happiness, well-being, and mood will all improve. Studies have proven that this kind of meditation can prevent depression and improve anxiety and stress levels. You will learn how to deal with irritability and emotional stressors more easily. Many other studies have proven that people that meditate won't see their doctors as often as others, and won't spend as much time in hospitals.

Your memory will also improve and you will have a faster reaction time.

Even though there are lots of benefits to mindfulness, that have been proven, people are still leery of the word meditation. Let's look at some myths of mindfulness.

Mediation and religion are not the same thing. Mindfulness is a way to train your mind. Lots of religious people practice meditation, but agnostics and atheists meditate as well.

There is no need to sit on the floor, cross-legged, but that is an option. You can also sit in a chair to meditate. Mindfulness is not limited to where you sit. You can bring it to wherever you are, train, bus, car, or walking. You are able to meditate wherever you are.

Meditation does not take up a bunch of your time. It does, however, take some persistence and patience. Lots of people realize that meditation can liberate them from the worry and stress of time. They find that they have more time to spend on more fun things in their life.

Mindfulness meditation does not have to be hard. It is also not about failure or success. You will have times when it feels difficult, but even then you will learn something from the experience. You learn how your mind works, giving you psychological benefits.

It won't make your mind go numb causing you to veer off of your lifestyle or career goals. You also won't become some brainwashed follower. It doesn't mean you have to accept the unacceptable. It only means that you will be able to see the world in a clearer way. It allows you to be wiser and take more knowledgeable actions in your life and allows you to be able to see a smarter path for your goals.

Basically, when you are mindful you are:

Not judging things that you notice, and you don't label things

You concentrate on the things that are around you on purpose

You try to avoid thinking about the things that have happened, or that might happen to you

You focus on the present

Humans spend so much of their life thinking about things that have already happened, trying to find ways that they could have avoided something, or constantly worrying about things to come, that they aren't able to appreciate what is right in front of them. Mindfulness gives you the ability to bring yourself to the present moment. You will be able to:\s

Cope with your stressors and stress

Relax

Concentrate more fully

Slow the nervous system

Slow down the thought process

Become more aware of the environment, body, and yourself

Clear the head\sWho Can Mindfulness Help

Mindfulness is a practice that anybody can develop, and anybody is able to try it. It has been in practice for thousands of years and has spread across the world. Anybody is able to increase mindfulness within their life through yoga and meditation, or by paying attention to things while doing regular everyday activities like brushing your teeth.

If you are continually battling neck, back, or other physical issues, a portion of the problem may be psychological. According to a 2011 research, 80 minutes of mindfulness may almost halve the experience of pain.

Another research conducted by the University of Montreal corroborates this. They evaluated 13 meditators who had all completed 1,000 hours or more of meditation and compared them to non-meditators to see if meditation had any influence on pain perception. Finally, the meditators had a higher pain threshold than the others.

Microbiome of the Gut

If you weren't previously aware, your body is now infested with microorganisms. These are the microbes that comprise your microbiome. The majority of these bacteria reside in the gut or large intestine. When your microbiome becomes imbalanced or altered, you may suffer weight gain, impaired immunity, and inflammation.

They discovered a link between stress hormones and psychological stress, as well as their influence on microbial alterations in the intestines, in a few modest investigations. This indicates that mindfulness-based stress reduction may be able to prevent detrimental microbiota alterations.

Symptoms of Irritable Bowel Syndrome

IBS is a widespread ailment that affects around 7% to 10% of the world's population. Nobody knows for certain what causes IBS, but experts feel that it is likely caused by a combination of events. They hypothesize that psychological distress, stress, and digestive imbalances may be to blame.

Given that mindfulness may assist with all three likely primary triggers, it seems reasonable that it can assist in managing IBS. In a study of 43 patients, it was discovered that those who received mindfulness training saw a greater decrease in their symptoms. Even six months later, the advantages remained.

Diseases of the Nervous System

According to a study conducted by doctors at Beth Israel Deaconess Medical Center, the brain alterations associated with mindful meditation may help prevent the advancement of cognitive illnesses such as Alzheimer's and dementia. After eight weeks of mindfulness stress reduction, the Alzheimer's patients in the research had a slower deterioration in cognitive capacities than the control group. Additionally, they demonstrated a rise in well-being, which aids in recuperation.

Pregnancy

Stress during pregnancy has been linked to a variety of unfavorable outcomes, including low birth weight, preeclampsia, and hypertension. Several studies have shown that it may help alleviate pregnancy-related stress.

In a five-week trial of 74 pregnant women, a portion of the participants got twice-weekly mindfulness sessions. They demonstrated a greater decrease in stress than the other group.

Chapter Three

Creativity

The two primary factors that influence your degree of creativity are convergent thinking, which involves cementing ideas into concepts, and divergent thinking, which involves coming up with new ideas. Lorenza Colzato and colleagues examined the impact of a variety of various meditation styles on these two primary cognitive processes. They discovered that all forms of meditation enhanced both convergent and divergent thinking.

The sort of meditation had an effect on the style of thinking. Free association meditation aided in the development of divergent thinking, whereas focused attention meditation aided in the development of convergent thinking.

Cancer

In 2012, there were 14.1 million cancer cases worldwide. They anticipate a 68 percent rise in new cases by 2030. Mindfulness may aid in the management of cancer-related side effects and symptoms. Sleep quality, energy, anxiety, exhaustion, sadness, and stress are all affected. Recent research indicates that mindfulness may aid in the advancement of cancer therapy, particularly in breast cancer.

They are currently investigating why it works, but feel it has to do with stress management. In one research, 128 breast cancer patients were investigated, ranging from stage one to stage three:

Eight 90-minute mindfulness workshops and a six-hour retreat were offered to 53 patients.

For 12 weeks, 49 patients attended a 90-minute supportive-expressive therapy session once a week.

Only one six-hour stress management class was attended by 26 patients.

When they compared the three groups, they discovered that the third group had shorter telomeres after their intervention. Telomeres are responsible for protecting the DNA structure. Telomere length is associated with increased mortality and disease progression in cancer patients, particularly those with leukemia and breast cancer.

This is fantastic news, but bear in mind that this is still an ongoing study, and further research is necessary to determine the effectiveness of this treatment. Cancer therapy should not be limited to mindfulness.

The potential advantages of a consistent mindfulness practice are astounding. It's a rather innocuous habit, and one that you should engage in, given its potential adverse effects.
SUGGESTIONS

As I previously said, mindfulness practice is about exercising control over one's thoughts. You will learn how to live in the now and how to direct your attention to what you want, rather than what your mind desires. I'll discuss several mindfulness techniques you may incorporate in this chapter.

They use sitting meditation to cultivate awareness within Contemplative Psychotherapy and the Buddhist tradition. Additionally, there are numerous styles of meditation; some are used to relax, while others are used to induce altered states of consciousness.

Mindfulness is distinct from them all because it is not attempting to transform you into someone you are not. Rather than that, it assists you in recognizing what is genuine and present.

When meditation, there are three primary components to consider: thoughts, breath, and body. To begin, you have a relationship with your body. This also includes the way your environment is configured. Meditation is utilized to assist you in preparing to work with people, ensuring that you approach the situation with an open mind. That is why it is important to evaluate your surroundings. Most individuals are unable to dedicate a whole room to meditation, so they dedicate a corner or a few small locations in their house to practice. You may create a little altar and adorn it with various images and spiritual things if you choose. Additionally, incense and candles are excellent additions that may help establish the atmosphere. As long as you are not seated in front of a source of distraction such as a computer or television.

After you've established your meditation area, you'll want to establish a seat. This might be a floor cushion or a chair. If you prefer a cushion, you may purchase a gomden or zafu that are specifically intended for meditation, or you can use a folded blanket or pillow. The critical point is to have a secure seat that does not wriggle you about.

If you're going to use a chair, ensure that it's not too far back. If you are short enough that your feet swing when you sit in a chair, you should set something on the floor to rest your feet. When the legs dangle, the meditation becomes uncomfortable. If you are tall and have long legs, raise your hips slightly over your knees. That also applies to sitting on a cushion, since your back will begin to pain very fast without one.

Once everything is in place, take a seat and make yourself at home. Maintain an erect and straight posture, but avoid becoming stiff. The back is stretched upward, and a natural curve is maintained in the lower back. Consider the spine to be a tree and rest on it.

If you choose to sit on a cushion and cross your legs in the most comfortable position, you are not required to adopt an unpleasant posture. Hips must be higher than knees. If necessary, use an additional towel or blanket to lift your hips.

Gently place your palms on your thighs. Maintain a slight acuity in your eyes and focus on a spot on the floor in front of you. Allow your gaze to rest on the wall in front of you. Maintain a relaxed look. It is not directed towards a certain spot; it is more akin to looking out into space. It should simply be left alone.

Begin by just sitting in the setting you've created. If your mind begins to wander, gently bring it back to the present moment. It's normal for your mind to wander, which is why you must gently bring it back to the present.

The second component of mindfulness practice is awareness of one's breath. When you next begin to meditate, after you've found a comfortable position, pay attention to your breath quietly. Take note of how it feels when you inhale and exhale. You are not required to take any special action. You are concentrating entirely on how you are now breathing, rather than on how you may alter your breath. Allow yourself to breathe freely if you become aware that you are regulating your breathing. It will be challenging at first, so try not to concentrate on whether or not your breath is natural.

For a few minutes, sit in your setting and posture, paying attention to your breath. As it enters and as it exits. Your emphasis should be around 25% on your breath. It is not about getting it just correct, but about being aware that your attention is not entirely focused on the breath itself. 75% of your focus should be on the environment and body.

The third component of mindfulness practice is to pay attention to one's thoughts. While seated and meditating, you will notice that ideas will arise. At times, numerous ideas will overlap. These might be dreams, plans, recollections, television ad jingles, or fantasies. You may feel as if you are unable to concentrate on your breath due to your thoughts. This is a regular occurrence, particularly among newcomers to meditation. The critical point is to pay attention to how you feel.

When you get so involved in your thoughts that you lose track of your surroundings, gradually return your focus back to your breathing. If it helps, you may convince yourself that you were thinking. This is not a judgment; it is just a way of describing what you were doing.

Now that you understand what a fundamental practice is, you undoubtedly want to know how long to practice for. If you are a total novice, begin with ten to fifteen minutes each day or every other day and gradually advance to twenty to thirty minutes. You may even practice for 45 minutes to an hour if you are highly proficient. If you want to meditate for an extended period of time, it may be beneficial to learn how to conduct walking meditation as a way to break up your practice.

It's important to keep in mind that mindfulness is about developing the ability to be attentive of oneself. It is not a matter of restraining your thoughts and compelling yourself to stop thinking. Many would believe that is the objective, but it is not. While certain meditations may attempt to silence your thoughts, this is not what mindfulness is about. When you catch yourself thinking, which you will, pay attention to it. Avoid attempting to eradicate them, since this would be the polar opposite of what mindfulness is about. You're attempting to be who you are at the time. You are not attempting to transform into someone else.

Here is a step-by-step guide to establishing a mindfulness meditation practice.

Choose a meditation location: choose a space in your home that you can dedicate exclusively to meditation practice. Personalize it with cushions, photographs, candles, and incense. Prepare to be comfortable: meditation will take at least ten minutes, and you will not want to be trapped in clothing that pinches and binds, causing discomfort. Additionally, ensure that the space is at a temperature that is pleasant for you. Keep additional blankets and pillows on hand in case you need them. Set aside time: if you have guests, inform them of your plans and request that they refrain from disturbing you during your meditation time. Set a timer on your phone for the duration of your meditation. This should begin at ten minutes and then be increased as needed. Different postures: While the majority of people believe that you must sit in lotus with crossed legs to meditate, this is not true. Sit in various postures or even lie down. This modifies the situation in such a way that you

don't get your practice bores you. Begin by calming your thoughts and letting go of the past. This might be difficult if you've had a particularly stressful day or if you're new to the sport. You could even notice that emotions are beginning to surface. This is all very natural and acceptable. Take a few deep breaths and become aware of the sensation of breathing. Take notice of the temperature of your breath as it passes down your neck and into your lungs. You are not your ideas: when you meditate, thoughts will arise; however, they will not have influence over you; rather, you will have control over them. Recognize and release negative ideas and feelings as they arise. Breathe: if you feel distracted, return your attention to your breath. Breath is the heart of your being. It is the constant to which you may return anytime anything attempts to seize control of your thinking. The present moment: the purpose of mindfulness is to cultivate an awareness of the present moment. When the mind naturally wanders to the past or future, you must bring it back to the present now.

After you've mastered the fundamentals of mindfulness meditation, let's consider some more methods to incorporate mindfulness into your life.

Observe

Maintain an awareness of your focal point. Allow your thoughts to wander unless you are really interested in doing so. Make an effort to think about things intentionally rather than being absent-minded. It's easy to get absorbed in the stress of daily life, but it's critical to check in and ensure that you're paying attention to what you're doing.

Keep a close eye on your actions. While mindfulness and awareness are inextricably linked, they are not synonymous. Being cognizant of the fact that you are having a discussion is not synonymous with being careful of how you speak to someone. Keep a record of everything you say and do, as well as the reasons behind your actions. As I indicated before, the majority of individuals float through life on autopilot, responding and reacting as necessary. Being ability to check in with oneself and be aware of the rationale for your actions.

Everything you do should be purposeful. Attending to everything that happens around you and where you are is the act of giving everything meaning. Giving something a purpose may take on a variety of forms. This may imply giving something your undivided attention or being mentally present while doing tasks.

Present-Oriented Living

Maintain a sense of present-tenseness. It is quite common for people to begin focusing on past events. This has a detrimental effect on your mental health and well-being. When you become aware of your thoughts drifting to the past, redirect them to the present. Take the time to learn from your mistakes and then move on.

Avoid becoming absorbed in future-oriented thoughts. Everybody has to consider their future occasionally, but when these thoughts begin to interfere with daily life, they become an issue. Mindfulness entails thinking about and living in the present moment, rather than in the future. Make the necessary future plans, but avoid becoming consumed by the 'what ifs'. You will be incapable of appreciating what occurs in your daily life.

Put your watch away. Many people in the modern world have developed a reliance on some type of clock. Individuals are constantly checking their watches or cell phones to determine the time and the amount of time remaining until they have to do something. You must learn to live in the moment rather than relying on the passage of time. It's acceptable to check the time, but you must avoid becoming entangled in the flow of time.

Allow for periods of inactivity. While it is critical to be productive, you must also allow for personal time. Allow yourself some alone time throughout the day. Meditation is a practice that entails sitting quietly and letting go of past events. This provides an opportunity for you to de-stress and unwind.

Allow Judgment to Pass You By

Negative emotions and judgments should be let go of. When you bring your thoughts back to the present moment, you will notice things you have never noticed before. Observing things you haven't noticed before is a component of being mindful. You must develop the ability to observe these events objectively and without attaching any blame or emotion to them. Accept them, learn from them, and then keep moving forward.

Make an effort not to cling to happy feelings. This may seem counterintuitive, but mindfulness is not solely concerned with happiness. Through the practice of mindfulness, you can transcend negative or positive emotions. If you live in the present moment, you can appreciate the good things that have happened in your life without being concerned about how they will end. If you compare your current positive moments to your previous positive moments, you will find that you are not as appreciative of the present.

Consider your emotions in the same way that you would a storm. Mindfulness is about living in the present moment and letting go of all judgments, expectations, regrets, and fears. This is not to say that you must be emotionless. Rather than that, you must embrace your emotions and then allow them to pass, as a rain storm does. You have no control over the weather, and similarly, you have no control over your feelings about certain aspects of life.

Compassionate and kind to those in your immediate vicinity. You must be present without judgment, but you must also recognize that others may not share your beliefs and emotions. You will encounter times when you must associate with individuals who obsess over negative emotions or are simply going through a difficult time. Simply because you are able to let go of the past and future does not mean you are able to disengage from the world around you. You should make an effort to be empathetic toward those around you.

PRACTICES PERFORMED EVERY DAY

While you now understand how to begin your own mindfulness meditation practice, you may be wondering how to incorporate mindfulness into your daily life. You may also be disinclined to begin a meditation practice, but a few simple actions can help you incorporate mindfulness into your life.

As you have discovered, humans have a tendency to operate on autopilot, which occurs more frequently when performing routine daily tasks. This is the time to practice mindfulness. You are not required to clear your mind of all thoughts; simply become aware of your actions and how they feel. Here are some activities that will help you develop a greater awareness of your surroundings.

Vacuuming

When you're operating on autopilot, you're only dimly aware of the sensation of the water as you shower. You struggle to get the water just right, to reach the desired temperature, but your mind wanders to what you saw on television or what you have to do today. You are not currently residing in the present moment.

Rather than that, consider the temperature of the water and how it feels as it slides down your body. Consider the scent and feel of your shower gel, shampoo, conditioner, or soap. Once you're accustomed to noticing these details, being more mindful will become second nature.

Maintain good oral hygiene.

You probably don't consider what you're doing when you brush your teeth. You've been doing it for years, and it isn't particularly difficult. You fix your gaze on your reflection, more concerned with the appearance of your skin than with the task at hand. You may even have to sprint around the house with the toothbrush protruding from your mouth.

Rather than that, concentrate on the toothpaste's texture and flavor. Consider the sensation of the brush in your mouth as you move it. Consider the sensations created by the floor beneath your feet and the movement of your arm. Brushing your teeth should be done with caution.

To work, drive

You climb into your car, bus, or train and stare out the window mindlessly. Even when you're driving, you're not paying attention to what's going on around you; you're preoccupied with what you're about to do. The man sitting next to you on the bus falls asleep on your arm and you are unaware until it is time to exit.

Rather than that, focus on the people in your immediate environment. Whether you drive or take public transportation, take notice of your surroundings, their appearance and aroma. Take note of the ride's characteristics; is it rough or smooth? What do you pass? Take note of minor details that you might have missed previously.

Chapter Four

Dishwasher cleaning

Although the majority of people now own a dishwasher, when forced to wash dishes by hand, they moan as they approach the sink. You scrub, rinse, and dry robotically; and you do so repeatedly.

Rather than that, pay attention to the sensations. On your hands, feel the water. Take note of how the scrubber feels against the dishes as you rub it. Consider how dirty dishes feel in comparison to clean dishes.

Form a queue

There are numerous instances when you will find yourself in line; at the grocery store, shopping mall, or DMV, for example. You stand there, avoiding eye contact and muttering under your breath about how long it's taking.

Rather than that, begin observing and observing. Take note of the neighborhood's true appearance. Consider your surroundings; avoid staring as this may offend others. Take note of the odors; they should be pleasant. Utilize this opportunity to become more aware of your surroundings.

Apart from paying attention to the mundane tasks you perform on a daily basis, you can begin incorporating additional actions into your life that will gradually increase your mindfulness. I've included a few examples below. Consume consciously

When you eat without thinking about what you're doing, whether on your phone or while watching TV, you miss out on the joy of eating. You have no sensory perception of the food's flavor. You are olfactory deaf. Additionally, it may cause you to feel sated and full. This is because your mind believes you have skipped a meal because no other sensory triggers were present. Make a conscious effort not to multitask while eating. When it's time to eat, sit down and concentrate entirely on your food. Walk with intention.

While walking may appear to be a necessity for getting around, it is much more. While walking, take note of how it feels. Take note of your body's movements and the objects in your immediate environment. Take note of how your feet make contact with the ground and the muscles required to pick them up. While walking, take note of the sounds and sights you encounter. Bear in mind your breath.

Breathing is a natural occurrence that is rhythmical. When you take the time to notice it, it will anchor your mind in the present moment and put an end to your mind's wandering thoughts for a brief moment. For several minutes, you are free of your own thoughts. At that moment, as you contemplate your breath, you are free of all fears and concerns; you are simply present. Your senses will thank you

Utilize all of your senses, including sight, touch, sound, smell, and taste. These provide access to the present moment. When you are completely immersed in your head, your senses are rendered inactive. If you've ever heard the expression "stop and smell the roses," then that is precisely what you should do. Take note of the aroma emanating from your coffee. At the beach, smell the salty air. Consider the variety and color of the flowers in your immediate vicinity. Take note of how the pizza smells and tastes. Sensitize yourself to the movement of your clothing. Smell and feel the freshly laundered bed sheets. The kiss of your significant other will fill you with warmth and comfort. Consider how grass feels beneath your feet. When you take a bath or wash your hands, the water has a certain feel to it. As you go about your day, utilize all of your senses. Throughout the day, pause.

Stop what you're doing and simply listen to your surroundings for a moment. Consider the sound of the phone ringing. Consider how your body weight feels in the chair in which you are seated. Before you open the door, give the door handle a gentle squeeze. Taking moments throughout the day to pause and center yourself can help you become more aware and mindful. Additionally, it allows for mental clarity and can provide an energy boost. Consider these pauses to be bookends for the tasks that will begin and end your day.

Heart-to-heart listening

As humans, we have a proclivity to overlook what others say when they speak to us. They are either preoccupied with what they are about to do or with something that has just occurred to them. Additionally, they may be judging what the other person is saying or may be lost in a daydream. When you next speak with someone, make a point of truly listening to what they have to say. Avoid becoming disoriented by thought. If you become distracted from their words, refocus your attention. You do not need to worry about what you will say in response; your mind will know what to say, and it is acceptable to pause for a moment after they finish speaking before you begin. Become absorbed in the activity you enjoy

Each of us has certain activities that we truly enjoy. They enable us to connect with our spirit and experience a sense of completeness. Swimming, cooking, construction, dancing, painting, hiking, gardening, singing, or writing are all examples of activities. What it is is irrelevant. You'll discover that when you engage in these activities, you'll lose yourself in them. This is not to say that you switch to automatic mode. You lose the part of yourself that is constantly concerned about things when you perform these tasks. It calms your mind because you are engaged in an activity that you enjoy and are entirely focused on the present moment. Increase your participation in these activities during the week to increase your happiness.

Daily meditation

Meditation has lots of benefits, many of which we have already covered. You will have more energy, inspiration, peace, and happiness. You don't have to have a lot of time to meditate. 10 minutes a day can positively affect your day to day life. This will also boost your mindfulness, so it will become easier to use mindfulness during your day. Mix up your day to day

There are lots of reasons why you feel so happy during the holiday season. When you travel to different places your mind will automatically become more mindful. This happens because there are new smells, sights, and sounds to experience. The senses naturally take over and it frees your mind so you can live in the moment. If you don't have time to travel somewhere, that's okay. You can get the same effect by switching up your normal day to day routine. Instead of driving the same way to work every day, change up your route. Try a different coffee shop. Shop in places you have never been in, or participate in some local adventure, or learn something new. Take notice of emotions and thoughts

You've heard me say this before; you are not your thoughts; you only observe your thoughts. Since you can listen to what your thoughts are, that proves they aren't you. You're separate from your thoughts. Simply acknowledging them and observing them without any judgment allows you to become more present in your life. This keeps you from getting caught up in the constant flow of your thoughts. When you take notice of your thoughts, avoid letting them carry you away. Think of the thought like a train. You're standing on the platform and you just watch as the trains come in and as they leave. You don't try to jump on them and let them take you to some unknown place. Traits of the Mindful Person

Mindful people are going to live their life differently than the autopilot person. Here are some ways to know if a person is a mindful person.

They take lots of walks.

It's easy in our crazy world to become burnout and exhausted, and the mindful person knows how to solve that problem. Through walking. They know that they can go on a walk to clear their mind and to help them calm their thoughts. A walk can give them more awareness and a new perspective. Also, being in nature and seeing all the greenery might actually be good for the brain and send it to a meditative space. Studies have shown that walking outside gives you the ability for involuntary attention, which means that your mind can focus on the present and you can also have the chance to reflect.

Daily tasks are done mindfully.

Like I mentioned earlier, taking a notice of the little things that happen during your normal tasks is a good way to be mindful. Noticing how things feel, taste, and smell brings you into the moment.

They create things.

Mindfulness can boost your creative ability. Mindful people will naturally start doing more creative things during their day. The act of creative work can help you place your mind in a meditative state. If you are having problems in regular meditation, doing something like drawing, cooking, or singing can help you meditate.

They listen to their breath.

I've covered this a lot. Mindful people notice everything about their breathing. They don't breathe on autopilot.

They don't multitask.

Multitasking will keep people from being able to focus on things that they are doing. It is the enemy of mindfulness. Most people, though, multitask throughout their whole day. Some studies have discovered that when a person's attention is divided between tasks, it will take them 50 percent longer to finish the task. Errors are also more likely to happen. You need to make sure that you only focus on one thing at a time. Interruptions will happen, but you have to bring yourself back to the one task at hand. They check their phone at the right time.

People who are mindful keep their relationship with electronics healthy. This could be making sure that as soon as they wake up they don't reach for their phone to check their e-mail. The same goes for bedtime too. They may even go so far as to keep their phone in a completely different room than the one that they sleep in. They may even turn it off on the weekends or on vacation so that they can unplug. The biggie is that they turn off their phones when they are with family and friends. This allows them to mindfully interact with the people around them.

They look for new experiences.

When meditation, there are three primary components to consider: thoughts, breath, and body. To begin, you have a relationship with your body. This also includes the way your environment is configured. Meditation is utilized to assist you in preparing to work with people, ensuring that you approach the situation with an open mind. That is why it is important to evaluate your surroundings. Most individuals are unable to dedicate a whole room to meditation, so they dedicate a corner or a few small locations in their house to practice.

You may create a little altar and adorn it with various images and spiritual things if you choose. Additionally, incense and candles are excellent additions that may help establish the atmosphere. As long as you are not seated in front of a source of distraction such as a computer or television.

After you've established your meditation area, you'll want to establish a seat. This might be a floor cushion or a chair. If you prefer a cushion, you may purchase a gomden or zafu that are specifically intended for meditation, or you can use a folded blanket or pillow. The critical point is to have a secure seat that does not wriggle you about.

If you're going to use a chair, ensure that it's not too far back. If you are short enough that your feet swing when you sit in a chair, you should set something on the floor to rest your feet. When the legs dangle, the meditation becomes uncomfortable. If you are tall and have long legs, raise your hips slightly over your knees. That also applies to sitting on a cushion, since your back will begin to pain very fast without one.

Once everything is in place, take a seat and make yourself at home. Maintain an erect and straight posture, but avoid becoming stiff. The back is stretched upward, and a natural curve is maintained in the lower back. Consider the spine to be a tree and rest on it.

If you choose to sit on a cushion and cross your legs in the most comfortable position, you are not required to adopt an unpleasant posture. Hips must be higher than knees. If necessary, use an additional towel or blanket to lift your hips.

Gently place your palms on your thighs. Maintain a slight acuity in your eyes and focus on a spot on the floor in front of you. Allow your gaze to rest on the wall in front of you. Maintain a relaxed look. It is not directed towards a certain spot; it is more akin to looking out into space. It should simply be left alone.

Begin by just sitting in the setting you've created. If your mind begins to wander, gently bring it back to the present moment. It's normal for your mind to wander, which is why you must gently bring it back to the present.

The second component of mindfulness practice is awareness of one's breath. When you next begin to meditate, after you've found a comfortable position, pay attention to your breath quietly. Take note of how it feels when you inhale and exhale. You are not required to take any special action. You are concentrating entirely on how you are now breathing, rather than on how you may alter your breath. Allow yourself to breathe freely if you become aware that you are regulating your breathing. It will be challenging at first, so try not to concentrate on whether or not your breath is natural.

For a few minutes, sit in your setting and posture, paying attention to your breath. As it enters and as it exits. Your emphasis should be around 25% on your breath. It is not about getting it just correct, but about being aware that your attention is not entirely focused on the breath itself. 75% of your focus should be on the environment and body.

The third component of mindfulness practice is to pay attention to one's thoughts. While seated and meditating, you will notice that ideas will arise. At times, numerous ideas will overlap. These might be dreams, plans, recollections, television ad jingles, or fantasies. You may feel as if you are unable to concentrate on your breath due to your thoughts. This is a regular occurrence, particularly among newcomers to meditation. The critical point is to pay attention to how you feel.

When you get so involved in your thoughts that you lose track of your surroundings, gradually return your focus back to your breathing. If it helps, you may convince yourself that you were thinking. This is not a judgment; it is just a way of describing what you were doing.

Now that you understand what a fundamental practice is, you undoubtedly want to know how long to practice for. If you are a total novice, begin with ten to fifteen minutes each day or every other day and gradually advance to twenty to thirty minutes. You may even practice for 45 minutes to an hour if you are highly proficient. If you want to meditate for an extended period of time, it may be beneficial to learn how to conduct walking meditation as a way to break up your practice.

It's important to keep in mind that mindfulness is about developing the ability to be attentive of oneself. It is not a matter of restraining your thoughts and compelling yourself to stop thinking. Many would believe that is the objective, but it is not. While certain meditations may attempt to silence your thoughts, this is not what mindfulness is about. When you catch yourself thinking, which you will, pay attention to it. Avoid attempting to eradicate them, since this would be the polar opposite of what mindfulness is about. You're attempting to be who you are at the time. You are not attempting to transform into someone else.

Here is a step-by-step guide to establishing a mindfulness meditation practice.

Choose a meditation location: choose a space in your home that you can dedicate exclusively to meditation practice. Personalize it with cushions, photographs, candles, and incense. Prepare to be comfortable: meditation will take at least ten minutes, and you will not want to be trapped in clothing that pinches and binds, causing discomfort. Additionally, ensure that the space is at a temperature that is pleasant for you. Keep additional blankets and pillows on hand in case you need them. Set aside time: if you have guests, inform them of your plans and request that they refrain from disturbing you during your meditation time. Set a timer on your phone for the duration of your meditation. This should begin at ten minutes and then be increased as needed. Different postures: While the majority of people believe that you must sit in lotus with crossed legs to meditate, this is not true. Sit in various postures or even lie down. This modifies the situation in such a way that you

don't get your practice bores you. Begin by calming your thoughts and letting go of the past. This might be difficult if you've had a particularly stressful day or if you're new to the sport. You could even notice that emotions are beginning to surface. This is all very natural and acceptable. Take a few deep breaths and become aware of the sensation of breathing. Take notice of the temperature of your breath as it passes down your neck and into your lungs. You are not your ideas: when you meditate, thoughts will arise; however, they will not have influence over you; rather, you will have control over them. Recognize and release negative ideas and feelings as they arise. Breathe: if you feel distracted, return your attention to your breath. Breath is the heart of your being. It is the constant to which you may return anytime anything attempts to seize control of your thinking. The present moment: the purpose of mindfulness is to cultivate an awareness of the present moment. When the mind naturally wanders to the past or future, you must bring it back to the present now.

After you've mastered the fundamentals of mindfulness meditation, let's consider some more methods to incorporate mindfulness into your life.

Observe

Maintain an awareness of your focal point. Allow your thoughts to wander unless you are really interested in doing so. Make an effort to think about things intentionally rather than being absent-minded. It's easy to get absorbed in the stress of daily life, but it's critical to check in and ensure that you're paying attention to what you're doing.

Keep a close eye on your actions. While mindfulness and awareness are inextricably linked, they are not synonymous. Being cognizant of the fact that you are having a discussion is not synonymous with being careful of how you speak to someone. Keep a record of everything you say and do, as well as the reasons behind your actions. As I indicated before, the majority of individuals float through life on autopilot, responding and reacting as necessary. Being ability to check in with oneself and be aware of the rationale for your actions.

Everything you do should be purposeful. Attending to everything that happens around you and where you are is the act of giving everything meaning. Giving something a purpose may take on a variety of forms. This may imply giving something your undivided attention or being mentally present while doing tasks.

Present-Oriented Living

Maintain a sense of present-tenseness. It is quite common for people to begin focusing on past events. This has a detrimental effect on your mental health and well-being. When you become aware of your thoughts drifting to the past, redirect them to the present. Take the time to learn from your mistakes and then move on.

Avoid becoming absorbed in future-oriented thoughts. Everybody has to consider their future occasionally, but when these thoughts begin to interfere with daily life, they become an issue. Mindfulness entails thinking about and living in the present moment, rather than in the future. Make the necessary future plans, but avoid becoming consumed by the 'what ifs'. You will be incapable of appreciating what occurs in your daily life.

Put your watch away. Many people in the modern world have developed a reliance on some type of clock. Individuals are constantly checking their watches or cell phones to determine the time and the amount of time remaining until they have to do something. You must learn to live in the moment rather than relying on the passage of time. It's acceptable to check the time, but you must avoid becoming entangled in the flow of time.

Allow for periods of inactivity. While it is critical to be productive, you must also allow for personal time. Allow yourself some alone time throughout the day. Meditation is a practice that entails sitting quietly and letting go of past events. This provides an opportunity for you to de-stress and unwind.

Chapter Five

What Are Chakras?

Allow Judgment to Pass You By

Mindful people are open to new things. People that prioritize peace of mind and presence will enjoy savoring the little moments and big moments in life. Having new experiences will make you more mindful as well.

They venture outside.

Making time to experience the outdoors is a powerful way to reboot your mind and give you a sense of wonder and ease. The outdoors can help you to relieve stress and boost energy and attention. You will find that your memory will become better after you have spent some time outside.

They know what they are feeling.

Contrary to popular belief, mindfulness isn't solely about being happy every moment of the day. Instead, it's about accepting what happens and how you feel. If you are constantly preoccupied with being happy, you are only hurting yourself in the long run. You will constantly focus on the fact that you are not happy, and that only causes you to be unhappy.

They take the time to meditate.

This has been talked about a lot. Meditation plays a large role in being mindful, and mindful people know and understand that.

They know the mind and body.

People tend to shove food in their mouth without thinking about how it tastes, or if it's making them feel full. Mindful people will make sure they notice everything about what they eat and how their body responds to it.

They don't take themselves seriously.

People like to worry about everything they have done and the problems they have. A mindful person doesn't do that. They keep their sense of humor even when there are problems going on in their life.

They allow their mind to wander.

Mindfulness is about being present, but letting your mind wander is also important. Mindful people are able to find that happy medium between mindful and autopilot. If you stay constantly present, you may miss out on connections between your mind and the world. Using your imagination may even help your mindfulness in the long run. CONCLUSION

Thank for making it through to the end of Transform Your Life Through Mindfulness, let's hope it was informative and able to provide you with all of the tools you need to achieve your goals whatever it may be.

The next step is to get started with your mindfulness practice. There's no time like the present to change your life. You have learned the benefits of mindfulness, and you have learned how to add mindfulness into your life, so there is no reason to wait any longer for great changes.

If you choose not to adopt a mindfulness meditation practice into your life, the least you can do is start adding mindfulness practices of different kinds into your everyday practices.

If there is only one thing that you get from this, let it be: Mindfulness is a practice that anybody can develop, and anybody is able to try it. It has been in practice for thousands of years and has spread across the world. Anybody is able to increase mindfulness within their life through yoga and meditation, or by paying attention to things while doing regular everyday activities like brushing your teeth.

Finally, if you found this book useful in any way, a review on Amazon is always appreciated!

Prior to being able to actually use the chakras for healing and other energy work, it is important to understand what they are and where they come from. When you are able to understand the history and origin of chakras, as well as what they are exactly, you will have a greater ability to understand why they are important and how they can help you. Establishing this foundation around the chakra knowledge will create a better basis for you to learn all about them throughout the rest of this book.

History and Origins

Back between 1500 and 500 BC within' the oldest Indian text of the Vedas, there was writing about the chakras. These chakras, then spelled "cakra", have also been referenced in other texts and history including the Cudamini Upanishad, the Shri Jabala Darshana Upanishad, the Shandilya Upanishad and the Yoga-Shikka Upanishad. The knowledge about the sophisticated chakra system passed through the Ino-European people through oral tradition. These people were also called Aryan. Traditionally, the chakra system was part of Eastern philosophy; however, New Age authors resonated deeply with the idea and made it more readily available to modern people through their text.

When you look at the very definition of a chakra, it is a spinning disk or a wheel. Essentially, a chakra is known to be a spinning disk on the human body that churns energy through it. The chakras run along the length of your spine, starting at the "root" chakra at the base of your spine, all the way to your "crown" chakra at the top of your head. There are seven primary chakras that run along this length of your body, though in some more sophisticated and in-depth texts you will read that there are as many as 114 throughout the entire body and energy field.

The primary chakras focused upon in spirituality and energy work and healing are the seven that run along the length of your spine. These chakras directly associate with the health of the physical body, mind, and emotions of a person. Because of this, many practices such as energy healing and yoga work closely with the chakras to create a powerful state of wellbeing for everyone who takes the time to engage in these activities.

What Do Chakras Do?

Expanding on the idea of chakras being spinning lights of energy over primary areas on the body, you can then grow to realize that each one has a unique purpose directly associated with the wellbeing of the body. Essentially, they govern the way we psychologically experience life when we are affected by mental and emotional stimuli. Each spinning disc contributes to our overall wellbeing, and we can directly experience what our chakra experiences, whether it is open, closed, balanced or unbalanced, active or inactive, so on and so forth. When you work with these chakras to have them operating in a healthy flow, you will find that your wellbeing physically, emotionally and mentally is much more positive overall. You can drastically alter your state of being through the chakras, and therefore working with them has a powerful ability to heal your energetic, physical and spiritual beings. When you release any blockages within' the chakra and balance them so that they work in healthy flow, you give yourself the ability to flow easily through a healthy, enlightened and balanced existence. The balance within' our chakras

directly correlates with the balance in our own personal lives, physically, mentally and emotionally. Working with them can assist you in eliminating many unwanted ailments you may be suffering from.

What Else Do I Need to Know About Chakras?

Each chakra is located in a different spot along your spine and serves a different purpose. They also affect different organs and correlate with different ailments. Each one has its own color. They also directly relate to their own set of emotions, feelings, and behaviors. Each one can be worked on to heal the ailments that directly associate with it, once you realize which one is unbalanced or out of alignment.

The chakras are a very sophisticated map of the energy body and directly affect our physical, mental and emotional bodies as well. They were first depicted in text sometime between

1500 of 500 BC in some of the oldest texts in the world. Chakras offer a powerful opportunity for you to learn how you can balance your body and heal many ailments that you may struggle or suffer fro. When you do, you will likely find that your entire wellbeing is much better off for it. CHAPTER 2: THE SEVEN CHAKRAS

As you learned in the previous chapter, there are seven primary chakras that you should consider. While some people believe there are up to 114, most people simply focus on these primary seven. Each chakra governs its own set of feelings, emotions, organs, and behaviors. They also have their own color and placement on the bottom. Within' this chapter, we are going to go deeper into the knowledge on each of the seven chakras. We will start with the one at the bottom of your spine known as the "root chakra" and work our way up to the one at the top of your spine called the "crown chakra". This order takes us from the first to the seventh chakra. Along the way, you will learn all that you need to know about each one.

The Root Chakra

The first of all of the seven chakras is the Root Chakra. This bright red chakra is located at the base of your spine, between your legs. In some texts or teachings, this chakra is associated with an Earthy brown tone, instead of a red one.

The Root Chakra is responsible for feeling grounded and stable in your life, as well as feeling a sense of security. The most common signal that this chakra is unaligned is a feeling of anxiety. You can experience this symptom whether this chakra is under or over active. If you are experiencing an underactive Root Chakra, you will also experience feelings of being unsafe or afraid in your life. If it is overactive, you may be feeling stuck in your ways or struggle to accept transition or change within your life. Either way, the best method for balancing this chakra is to meditate and practice grounding techniques. In doing so, you will help alleviate many of the ailments that arise with it.

This chakra directly associates with the organs such as your kidney, reproductive glands and organs, and your spine. If you are experiencing any difficulties such as kidney infections or pain, difficulty reproducing or with reproductive hormones, or pain in your spinal column, it may be due to your Root Chakra being misaligned. You can likely restore balance to your chakra and experience reduced stress in any of these systems.

The Sacral Chakra

The second of the seven chakras is the Sacral Chakra. This chakra is located above the pelvis in between your hips. This chakra resonates with the color orange.

The Sacral Chakra is responsible for your passion, sexuality and your creativity. When you are experiencing an underactive Sacral Chakra, you may struggle to create, feel apathetic or rigid, or feel as though you are closed off from intimacy. When this chakra is extremely underactive, you may experience not only a lack of intimacy physically but emotionally as well. Alternatively, if this chakra is overactive you may feel as though you are extremely sexual to the point that you may be considered somewhat of a sex addict. You may also find that you tend to become emotionally attached easily, as well. Either way, you need to take the time to balance your Sacral Chakra. You can do so through meditation, mindfulness, and using some of the natural methods discussed later within' this book.

This chakra is directly associated with the organs such as your gallbladder, adrenal glands, immune system, waste organs, metabolism, and your spleen. When you are experiencing ailments within' any of these chakras, you should take the time to bring balance back to your Sacral Chakra. In doing so, you will likely eliminate a large amount of your negative side effects

and symptoms.

The Solar Plexus Chakra

The third chakra is the Solar Plexus Chakra and once again it's placement may seem obvious. It is located at the solar plexus, just above the belly button. This golden yellow chakra is a powerful one that resonates deeply with many areas of our lives.

The Solar Plexus Chakra is responsible for feelings of self-confidence, will, personal power and force. When you are feeling any misalignment within' the chakra, the emotional drawbacks will be difficult to manage. With an underactive Solar Plexus Chakra, you will find that you are feeling powerless, timid, or under confident within' yourself. If you are feeling low self-esteem, it is often associated with this chakra, as well. You may also lack direction or purpose within' your life. If this chakra is overactive, you may find that you are potentially aggressive or domineering and that you tend to try and be the "boss" of situations. Either is something that you should not strive for. Bringing balance to this chakra will assist you in feeling more confident and empowered without feeling as though you have to become overpowering.

The organs associated with the Solar Plexus Chakra include the upper spine, liver, stomach, pancreas, and metabolism. When this chakra is unbalanced, you may experience pain or ailments within' any of these systems. When you bring balance to the chakra, it is likely that each will function more efficiently and that your overall wellbeing will be enhanced by it.

The Heart Chakra

The fourth of the seven chakras is the Heart Chakra. This chakra is associated with the color green and is located directly in the center of your rib cage. As you may assume, it is located exactly where your heart is. Some people call this chakra the

"Heart Center". The two appear to be used interchangeably throughout text regarding energy healing and the energy body. In this book, we will call it the Heart Chakra.

The Heart Charka is primarily responsible for feelings of love and compassion. When you are experiencing an underactive Heart Chakra, you may find that you struggle to feel love or compassion for people and things in your life. You may even struggle to experience these emotions for yourself. If your Heart Chakra is overactive, you may find that you love and give compassion freely to the point that you become clingy or overly affectionate towards people. If either of these situations is happening, you need to balance your Heart Chakra. You can do so by taking the time to go inward and discover what is causing you to be one way or the other. Often, we are affected by emotional experiences in our lives that cause us to be extremely cold or extremely affectionate towards others.

This chakra directly correlates with the heart organ, the lungs, and the thymus. If you are experiencing ailments in either of these, you may wish to do some energy balancing work with your heart chakra to restore balance and harmony within' them. Doing so may bring relief from

any ailments that bother you.

The Throat Chakra

As you may have guessed, the fifth chakra which is known as the Throat Chakra is located within' the throat. The color that correlates with this chakra is a bright and vibrant blue color. Typically, it is seen as more of a light blue color, though you may see it represented as nearly any shade of blue.

This chakra is responsible for honest communication and ease of self-expression. When this chakra is underactive, you may experience symptoms of being withdrawn, or even frustration, sadness, or anger due to feeling as though you are not speaking your truth. Alternatively, if it is overactive you may speak excessively and fail to filter yourself to the point that you may be seen as bossy or rude. Or, you may be a bad listener and you may listen merely for the opportunity to speak back. When you are experiencing either of these sets of symptoms, it is important that you take the time to develop a mindfulness practice and allow yourself to regain control over your voice. You should work on being honest if you are feeling as though you are hiding your truth, or you should work on keeping thoughts to yourself or learning to censor yourself if you are giving information or opinions too freely to the point that it is inhibiting your life.

The Throat Chakra is associated with the respiratory system, thyroid, and all organs that are associated with your throat and mouth. If you are experiencing any ailments with these organs, you may be experiencing physical symptoms of an unbalanced chakra. The most commonly reported symptom is feeling as though you have a lump in your throat. You can eliminate or ease these symptoms by restoring balance to your throat chakra and speaking your truth without over speaking.

The Third Eye Chakra

The Third Eye Chakra is located directly between and slightly above your eyebrows. This chakra is indicated by the color indigo and is considered to be the sixth of the seven chakras. For many, this is the most popularly recognized chakra as it is spoken about in many texts and spiritual teachings.

The Third Eye Chakra is responsible for bringing connection to intuition, psychic vision, and insight. When you are experiencing an underactive chakra, you may struggle to stay in touch with your intuitive side, or you may feel lost and as though you are wandering through life. Alternatively, if it is overactive, you may feel paranoid about your gut instincts and overanalyze things that are completely ordinary in life. To balance this chakra, you will want to meditate. Your meditation can have the intention of relaxing the chakra, or of opening it up depending on whether it is underactive or overactive. As a result, it should bring you back into a healthy flow where you can acknowledge and listen to your intuition without developing any fear or paranoia around the information that it brings you.

Physically, the Third Eye Chakra is associated with your pineal gland, pituitary gland, eyes, hormones and your brain. If you are experiencing misalignment in this chakra, you could experience a number of ailments with either of these organs. You may get headaches behind your eyes or experience disturbances in vision, you may get frequent headaches or "brain fog", you could experience hormonal changes that disrupt your wellbeing, or you could experience overactive or underactive pineal and pituitary glands. Bringing balance back to this chakra should be able to assist you in healing these ailments.

The Crown Chakra

Located on top of your scalp at the very top of your head, your Crown Chakra corresponds with the color purple. However, some people believe this chakra corresponds with the color white. You can use either one that resonates with you, but for this book and these teachings we are going to use purple. This chakra is considered the seventh of the seven chakras.

The Crown Chakra is responsible for assisting people with wisdom, being in attunement with the universe, and connecting to the spiritual realm. When this chakra is underactive, you may feel disconnected from spirit and as though you are making a number of foolish decisions. When it is overactive, you may feel as though you have your head in the clouds and you have difficulty connecting with reality. Neither of these are positive symptoms to have, so it is important that you bring balance back to the chakra to heal them. When it is functioning optimally, you will be able to have a healthy connection to the spiritual realm while still feeling firmly grounded in your life. If the chakra is overactive, you will want to ground yourself to bring yourself back down to Earth. If it is underactive, you will want to meditate and set the intention to reopen your ability to interact with the spiritual realm.

This chakra is responsible for governing the brain, the pineal gland, your biological cycles, and the spinal cord. When it is out of balance, you may experience ailments to any one of these. Your pineal gland may not function well, you may struggle to sleep well or you may sleep too much, you may experience pain in your spinal area or you may experience "brain fog" or frequent headaches. If you are noticing a number of these ailments or any single one that appears to be persistent and difficult to manage, you may want to consider healing and balancing your Crown Chakra. It may be unbalanced and bringing a lack of wellbeing to any of these areas.

When you see a map of the chakras, you may notice that they are coordinated in the colors of the rainbow. This knowledge is wonderful to note as it will assist you in remembering which color is associated with which chakra. Remember, red starts at the base and purple is at the top. Each chakra has its own color, emotions, behaviors and organs associated with it. When either is underactive or overactive or otherwise misaligned, you may experience symptoms associated with anything that your particular chakra is responsible for. If you are experiencing specific symptoms, you may want to revisit the chakras to see which one associates with where your symptoms are being felt. Then, you can do work with that chakra to bring peace and harmony to it and hopefully alleviate some or all of your symptoms.

CPSIA information can be obtained
at www.ICGtesting.com
Printed in the USA
BVHW061025130922
646893BV00007B/373